JACKIE KAY

FIERE

PICADOR

First published 2011 by Picador
an imprint of Pan Macmillan, a division of Macmillan Publishers Limited
Pan Macmillan, 20 New Wharf Road, London N1 9RR
Basingstoke and Oxford
Associated companies throughout the world
www.panmacmillan.com

ISBN 978-0-330-51337-1

5 7 9 8 6

A CIP catalogue record for this book is available from
the British Library.

Printed in the UK by CPI Group (UK) Ltd, Croydon, CR0 4YY

FIERE

Jackie Kay was born in Edinburgh. She is
a poet, novelist and writer of short stories and
has enjoyed great acclaim for her work for both
adults and children. Her novel *Trumpet* won the
Guardian Fiction Prize. The autobiographical
Red Dust Road won the 2011 Book of the Year at
the Scottish Book Awards and was shortlisted at
the Galaxy Book Awards. She has published two
collections of short stories, *Why Don't You Stop
Talking* and *Wish I Was Here*. She teaches at
Newcastle University and lives in Manchester.

Also by Jackie Kay

Red Dust Road

Wish I Was Here

Why Don't You Stop Talking

Trumpet

Poetry

The Lamplighter

Darling

Life Mask

Off Colour

Other Lovers

The Adoption Papers

For Ali Smith

And there's a hand, my trusty fiere
And gie's a hand o' thine

Robert Burns

Wherever someone stands,
something else will stand beside it.

Chinua Achebe

Fere, **feare**, **feer**, **fiere** or **pheere** (archaic)
noun: a companion, a mate, a spouse, an equal

Fere (Scot.)
adj: able, sound

Contents

FIERE

Fiere

If ye went tae the tapmost hill, fiere,
whaur we used tae clamb as girls,
ye'd see the snow the day, fiere,
settling on the hills.
You'd mind o' anither day, mibbe,
we ran doon the hill in the snow,
sliding and singing oor way tae the foot,
lassies laughing thegither – how braw,
the years slipping awa; oot in the weather.

And noo we're suddenly auld, fiere,
oor friendship's ne'er been weary.
We've aye seen the warld differently.
Whaur would I hae been weyoot my jo,
my fiere, my fiercy, my dearie O?
Oor hair it micht be silver noo,
oor walk a wee bit doddery,
but we've had a whirl and a blast, girl,
thru the cauld blast winter, thru spring, summer.

O'er a lifetime, my fiere, my bonnie lassie,
I'd defend you – you, me; blithe and blatter,
here we gang doon the hill, nae matter,
past the bracken, bonny braes, barley,
oot by the roaring sea, still havin a blether.
We who loved sincerely; we who loved sae fiercely,
the snow ne'er looked sae barrie,
nor the winter trees sae pretty.
C'mon, c'mon my dearie – tak my hand, my fiere!

I

Longitude

And though we share the same time
and we sleep and wake in unison
you are further away, in my dark mind;
odd times, I glimpse you walking
along the red dust road,
same age as me, same hands, feet, toes.
I anticipate where you are by
the light of the half moon in our sky,
but there is no starting position,
something else will have to be chosen.
When I look in the mirror
I don't see a foreign face,
no *Heart of Darkness*,
but you, who were with me all along,
walking that road not taken,
slowly, enjoying the elephant grasses,
holding my hand: two young lassies,
the breeze on our light-dark faces.

Night Moths

Last night when I opened my back door
ten red moths flew into my kitchen,
their paper wings, delicate as lanterns.
At night they came to light like motifs to folklore,
and now, suddenly ten, lined across my wall –
and kept so still: I wondered if they were ill.

I captured each visitor in an empty glass
– the ancestors come in many guises –
and took each one to the open door,
and watched as, under the one winged moon,
over the fence and into the starry sky,
the fluttering wings became a hello and goodbye.

The Returning

And when you came back, Matthew
– and your four-year-old body stopped its shaking –
and your temperature fell to nearly normal –
you had lost all your words: your soft mouth
silent as a rosebud, and your cheeks lit

like the sky after a double rainbow,
all your words flown like winter birds
as if the fit shook every new word
just learnt off your tongue;
and when you came back, Matthew, gift of god,

you could have come back as a girl,
your curly hair grown long in the space
you'd been gone, it seemed, and softer;
soft as the new beatific smile on your face,
benevolent, free of the world's wrongs.

I held your small shape reborn in my arms;
each eye shed a single tear, and I waited and held my breath.
And then I saw a silent word on your face and you were
back, and full of grace, back as if back
from the long-lost, the missing and the dead.

Igbo Bath

At first the bucket and the bowl in the bath
in the Beverley Hills Hotel, Nnewi,
perplexes me: maybe there's a leak
in the ceiling – but why is the bucket
upside down? I turn on the tap and it drips
slow-slow, till it dawns on me:
the bucket is to fill with water.
The bowl is to rinse.
When I tell all this to Chimamanda,
she laughs and says,
I should have told you about the Igbo bath,
and shares the joke with Chioma.

I took to the Igbo style of bathing
very quickly, splashing my bowl
of water under my arms, between my breasts,
down my legs and onto my feet,
building up a rhythm that felt
ancient, mythic, until I was
down by the river where the Odene bathed
daily, bent over, pouring the water over me,
years back, inside the body
of my grandmother; bathing the Igbo way
I am a split second, a spit and a jump away.

Granite

I found the quine and I found the loon
in the sparkling granite toon,
jist as the haar wis comin doon,
jist as the cloud had slaired the moon.

The faither's face is set in stane,
the mither cries and's all alane.
I've wandered richt up Gaelic Lane
doon Union Street and back agane.

Jist as granite comes fray *grain*,
gin they'll be grown folk search in vain,
tracking doon the past in the rain,
as lang as you'd ca' a stane a stane.

Brockit

Brockit: a zebra kens and maks sense
is unco proud o' its difference.

Brocked: the wee country, flecked wey charm,
black and white oats grow thegither.

Brucket: beauty and blethers,
dreich weather, mibbe sleekit pleassour in compliments.

Brockle: the bonny country, lined wey lochs, hills, glens, bens,
brooks, nooks, crannies, grannies.

Streak back through the lined time, find a' the brock-faced
beauties: balanced, waiting, biding time.

Ukpor Market

In the market in Ukpor
I saw a row of women
with my face: mirror image.
Same square physiognomy,
same wide nose, same broad smile.
The only difference I could see
was another shade of black.
Oyinbo! They say to me, *Oyinbo.*
I nod excitedly. Yes, my father
is an Igbo. *Oyinbo*, they say,
admiringly, touching my skin.
Onye Ocha. Kachi tells me
what they mean:
Oyinbo is a pidgin word
for white woman,
he says, smiling.

Egusi Soup

The first time I met my father, he ordered
hot pepper fish soup in the hotel bar
and told me his favourite soup was egusi
served with semo, eba or pounded yam.
His wife makes good egusi he tells me,
with stock fish, dry fish and crayfish,
with local Nsukka magi; with goat-meat
or beef-meat, and of course, pounded egusi,
protein-rich seeds of a large-seeded variety
of watermelon, fried in palm oil first –
be careful the oil doesn't splash – and you must
remove the bones from the dry fish and break
into big pieces, add chilli and pepper to taste.
For maximum flavour, add curry powder and thyme.
I like a lot of chilli, do you like things hot?
he asks me, *Then at the end, she throws*
in bitter leaf or ugwu or celerosia.
It helps if you have a cow's tongue,
something like that, or a beef or ox tail.

I told my father of a villager
quoted by Achebe who told his wife never
to give him egusi soup; so every evening the man
gets to eat his favourite soup, egusi, I say.
I see what you mean, I see what you mean, he says
laughing his laugh that is a little like mine.
Then, he put down his bowl and his spoon
as if he were from a fable or a fairytale,
a bear or a wood-cutter, a wolf in a frock
and vanished like a cow jumping over the moon,
or the dish running away with the spoon.

Body o' Land

Her eyes are the colour of Loch Ness
seen fray the tap o' the hill
coming doon the road fray Moniack Mhor.
Or the colour o' the field o' harebells
seen fray the train windae,
thru the Cairngorms, efter Aviemore.
She's no here nae mair,
but when I saw that hare
bound across the field by the wee bothy,
I thoucht of her, and then again efter
when the red deer stapped and stared
in Glen Strathfarrar, and late that nicht
when the crescent mune sang
a sweet lullaby tae the sky,
and then, next morn, early licht, first thing,
when the bricht yellow gorse smelt like her hair.
I saw her there, lying underwater for an aige,
her features thrawn and loose.
And then – aw o' a sudden – rising up,
her hair sleeked tae her heid,
like a seal, like a selkie.
There wis niver ony getting away.

Black River

We took a boat down the Black River,
the water darker than the darkest mirror,
the mangrove roots trailing the river bed –
as if searching for the dead down there.

We passed a tree shocked by the hurricane
whose spindly limbs had transformed
into a Rastafarian's dreadlocks,
rising from the river bed's rocks.

We passed crocodiles masquerading as logs
under the mangroves, and snow egrets
fluttering like blossom in the branches,
and the river carried us as if carrying us home –

wherever we were, wherever we came from:
a black river running through our arteries,
a black river putting our hearts at ease,
a black river touching our skin like a lover,

a black river to remind us of our ancestors,
running through the swamps and secret marshes
when freedom was a belief the river rushes
passed along the dark water like a breeze.

Then, later, when the river ran to meet the sea,
and the colours changed – black, to brown, to blue –
there was my son at the helm of the boat
as the boat lifted and crashed and smashed on the waves,

and there were the jack-fish leaping,
the dolphins' diasporic dive, and those strange birds
– whose name I have forgotten –
carrying an old song home.

Lament for the Mendi Men

That night out on the English Channel,
the fog was the colour of rice, of snow.
The Mendi sounded her whistles, moved slow.
The dark here was different from the African dark.
The fog carried the ghost's cloak of death,
a petrifying spectre, a spirit, a nightmare;
it was like nothing the men had ever seen before.
That night, they called for help and none came near.

Every man who sank down to the sea bed –
to be held by the sea bed's thick-lined body –
was a mother's son, a sister's brother, a lover's lover.
All the brothers lay silent at the bottom of the sea,
eleven miles south-west from St Catherine's light.
The hands of the ship's clock stopped; dark night.
The clock face stared blankly ahead. *Now, now;
it is time to remember the dead.*

Woman at a Window

(after the painting by Edgar Degas)

There's nothing in my appearance except that I am disappearing
into the uncertain light; nothing that would make me certain
of any conviction, or if I've made the right decisions in my life.
At this point, with my skin drinking in the available light,
I find it impossible to remember if I am widow or wife,
if I've had a life of ease, a life of strife. In the darkening

afternoon, nothing has happened and nothing will soon.
I am sitting at the window, forgetting the day I was born,
watching people come and go, unseen, invisible.
My hands are calm, steady on my lap. I am lying low.
Whatever it was that . . . ; I forget, the answer's no.
There is something slow and pleasing about disappearing

into the dissolving light. Nothing now will come to light.
Secrets I might have had will go with me to my grave.
Lovers I might have loved walk ahead, or are already dead.
I am sitting here at the window emptying my head
of the past or the future perfect, or the conditional.
I already know what is impossible, what's not been said.

In the room next to me, someone is playing a few bars
of an old piano; if I ever danced, I've forgotten
the steps; if I ever longed for change, I've lost
the path I meant to follow. Now, I am all shadow.
I sit at the window listening to the piano.
What was lost won't now come back. I've let it go.

Lady with a Parasol

(after Degas)

My master kept me in the dark, hidden for years.
I was not just his experiment, but I was his secret fear.
I understood him more than most: the dancers,
the woman drying herself after her bath.
We played a game where failure had its own allure,
over and over, through the afternoon and into the night.
I was forever at this racecourse, in the fading light,
backing a loser for the hundredth time.
Later, I realised it was losing I loved:
every black, white, or piebald horse I backed
was pipped to the post or fell at the first hurdle.
I stared at myself on my great master's wall.
I'd always be an unfinished *Lady with a Parasol*,
gambling with slim chances, who accepts
that life is gain and loss but mostly loss;
who has learnt not to show her face, and face up to it –
who knows all about the dying days, the missing, the lost,
who is never finished, never made,
who craves the lucky streaks of lost light: the shade.

from A Drunk Woman Looks at her Nipple

(after MacDiarmid)

I amna' fou sae muckle as tired – deid dune.
When I look closely at ma big bare breasts,
wee stars aroon a moon abune a toon,
my nipple's the spit o' the corona borealis.

Or my nipple's a galaxy, a milky way.
Look at whit we're daeing tae oor planet.
Whit's a planet but a lump o' rock, eh?
I've an affy feeling we're all for it.

Or my nipple's a wee castle surrounded by a moat.
We're burning holes in the ozone.
No aurora borealis, jist lactiferous ducts, blocked.
It's no that I'm sae fou, jist feeling a' alone.

I mind hoo the weans latched on this nipple,
aways the richt, niver the left,
till they made me hinkie-pinkie – yin fu, yin empty.
Yet this havering nicht; I'm bereft.

The milk that spilled wis creamy yellow, sandy dunes.
The colour o' the moon the nicht,
Areola borealis, the northern lichts o' auld Aberdeen.
The hole in the earth canna be seen.

In ain year, there's enough waste
tae fill dustbins stretching frae the earth to the mune.
I dinna ken as muckle's whaur I am
Or hoo I've come to sprawl here 'neth the mune.

Windows, Lakes

I always wanted a house with a bay window, my mother said,
reading the estate agent's window in Kendal.
*Imagine – sitting in the sun and reading a Simenon – heaven! –
in a cushioned bay window in an L-shaped room of a bungalow.*
It took me back to the houses of my mother's imagination long ago:
turrets and wings and open-plan kitchens –
space for Aga – conservatories, entrance halls,
ground-floor cloakrooms, *ooh la*, three double bedrooms
(one en-suite), dining, drawing and reception rooms.
Double-fronted Georgian townhouses, shutters and sash windows.
The years of window-shopping dream houses.
She never moved from her 1950s semi-detached Wimpey.

Wouldn't you have just loved a conservatory? she said,
peering at another: *4 beds, 350 grand –
grow cherry tomatoes, read the Sunday papers in the sun?*
All landscapes exist in the imagination, Naipaul said:
My mother's best houses were in her head.

I picked her up at Oxenholme, that nostalgic station.
I saw her searching for me through the train window.
She climbed gingerly onto the old platform,
William Morris walking stick in one hand, suitcase in another.
The train she got off sped into the past.

*

I drove my mother the scenic route to Carlisle
Through Staveley, past Beatrix Potter's Troutbeck,
Over the Kirkstone Pass – Grisedale to the west,
Beda Fall to the east, past Patterdale,
the tail end of Ullswater, Place Fell, Matterdale End,
Little Mell Fell gently waving hello,
snaking and winding our way, singing
You take the high road and I'll take the low
drinking it all in, the plains and vistas:
beautiful, beautiful, my mother said,
I always wanted to see the Lakes,

Wordsworth and Coleridge, Grasmere and Windermere.
But nothing compares to our Campsie Glens, our Fintry Hills,
she said, kissing my cheeks at Carlisle,
pulling herself onto the train for Glasgow,
too busy finding her seat with her stick and her bag to wave
through the window. I stood watching the train gather speed
along the track, until just the lines were left,
the double lines of the old train track.

I drove down the M6 back to Manchester,
past Penrith, the turn off to Kendal and Windermere.
I gripped the wheel, stared through the car window,
remembering the imaginary houses years ago:
the big bay window, bay horse and Play-Doh,
a half-open baby grand playing *fah soh lah ti doh*.

Strawberry Meringue

for Edwin Morgan

The time before the last time I saw you
my mum and I bought you a strawberry meringue,
a vanilla slice and a cream fancy
and round your bed we three
had our own wee tea party;
a nice auxiliary, Nancy, brought the tea,
and we thought of words to rhyme with meringue.
Did you say harangue? Am I right or am I wrang?

The old Home used to take you to Dobbies
on Mondays where they did marvellous meringues,
you said, your boyish eyes gleaming.
Then you asked me if I'd read Orhan Pamuk's
Snow, or *Red*, which was open on your bed,
and told me of a poem
you were translating from the Russian.
and asked after my son, and Carol Ann.
Love, you said. *Ah love*, wistfully.
If you can be friends you're doing not bad.

In your room today are perhaps a dozen books
and a few favoured paintings; life pared down,
clean as an uncluttered mind.
Friendship, dear Edwin, a scone, a meringue,
and your poems hovering like old friends too,
or old lovers – *Strawberries*, that last thrilling line –
was it *let the storm wash the plates*?
Nancy puts the rest of the cakes
in the fridge for you for later.
You are ninety! *Happy Birthday Edwin!*
Your head is buzzing with *Variations*,
And what is age but another translation?

Kamso, Kedu

Kamso Ozumba
You turned up on a Thursday,
in the middle of the nicht in February. Kedu?

Kamso Ozumba
Your braw face reflects wisdom from the auld yins.
When you came doon, the bricht stars shone, wee one.

Kamso Ozumba
You landit into love waiting for you here
from Chi Chi and Kachi, your mither and faither.

Kamso Ozumba
We'll put some whisky in the silver quaich
and bless your fine and handsome face. Slàinte mhath!

Between the Dee and the Don

'The middle ground is the best place to be.'
Igbo saying

I will stand not in the past or the future
not in the foreground or the background;
not as the first child or the last child.
I will stand alone in the middle ground.

I was conceived between the Dee and the Don.
I was born in the city of crag and stone.

I am not a daughter to one father.
I am not a sister to one brother.
I am light and dark.
I am father and mother.

I was conceived between the Dee and the Don.
I was born in the city of crag and stone.

I am not forgiving and I am not cruel.
I will not go against one side.
I am not wise or a fool.
I was not born yesterday.

I was conceived between the Dee and the Don;
I was born in the city of crag and stone.

I can say *tomorrow is another day* tomorrow.
I come from the old world and the new.
I live between laughter and sorrow.
I live between the land and the sea.

I was conceived between the Dee and the Don.
I was born in the city of crag and stone.

Fiere in the Middle

I was lost in the middle of my life;
I couldn't see the wood for the trees –
the silver birch, the beech, the sycamore.
It was summer: a chaos of leaves.
I went in further, deeper, than I'd been before.

I'd lost my way, my heart, my wife.
I couldn't read and I couldn't write.
Birds fell from branches. I lost my senses.
The dark came down and held me too tight.
I didn't want to be found; or let in the light.

You took the risk and cut through the forest.
You tracked one shoe and then another;
until you saw – as if from above, from further –
the haphazard symmetry of footsteps . . .
and you held my hand and led me out.

*

Then last year, it was you – lost in your middle years.
Your father died; your lover left in the coldest winter.
And the years you'd been there changed over; I was here.

The trees had no leaves, bare branches;
winter trees revered pure structure, odd symmetries.
Strange things happened on same days; coincidences.

I saw the girl you'd been; the old woman you'd be.
I came to your garden when no apples were on your trees;
I danced an African dance so your ghosts would leave.

Finding is an act of faith, you once said in the woods.
Should you be lost in the middle years . . .
the true fieres appear: *able, sound, equally good.*

Twins

(after Alice Neel)

We are the same; we are identical.
We are sitting on the piano stool;
our portrait is being painted by Alice Neel.
Be yourselves, don't feel obliged to smile.
Our mother stands behind Alice,
and looks at us being made on the canvas.
She says: *To think that parasitical nut*
helped create these beautiful girls!

We sit with our mouth shut tight;
we think the same thoughts in silent words.
That no-good, crazy, lackadaisical wretch,
our mother continues. *It takes two*, we think.
We share an arm and a red dress on the canvas,
white tights too. We dress the same;
a test of who can tell us apart.
I ought to have known he was no good

when he said he worked for Rentokil,
our mother is saying to Alice Neel
who laughs a maniacal laugh and says,
Yeah, but his face is fresh as paint.
And you can't ever bargain on a man's soul.
We keep our lips on the not-smile
against the lime-green wall. Our mother
says we are a miracle, but we make her

feel alone, *so damned alone sometimes.*
You won't need a mirror to watch
yourselves grow old, she says,
and then, bored waiting for us to be done,
lies down on Alice's chaise longue.
Are you going to be long with the twins?
I'm fed up looking at them:
it's the same face over again.

Burying My African Father

Now that I have walked all the way down
the red dust road and into Nzagha

and seen the lizards and geckos
and goats and all God's creatures

and walked beside the elephant grasses
the plantain, banana and cassava

through the gate of your compound
past the sign that read *Barbing Saloon here*

and held the tiny two-week-old baby
of your second cousin, and said *Odimma*

to her shy *Kedu*, and stood outside
your house and peered through the shutters,

and in the hotel room, I remembered you well
spinning and praying years ago in Abuja

when you told me you wouldn't reveal
the name of your village, your sons or your daughter.

Now that I have finally arrived, without you,
to the home of the ancestors, I can bid you farewell, *Adieu*.

For I must, with my own black pen – instead of a spade –
ashes to ashes and dust to dust,

and years before you are actually dead,
bury you right here in my head.

Limbo

Last night I felt myself crossing over
coming back from the dead –

The loved dead who are everywhere,
behind and up ahead.

Maybe the dead are loved more
than the living, I thought, light-headedly,

and I found myself skipping and singing
an old song from the store in my head.

The smells of the living
were stronger than anything I'd ever been fed.

The smell of sawdust from a small animal in a cage;
of a hyacinth in an old woman's kitchen window.

But I was out and back in the land of the living,
glad of the canny crocuses and daffodils, the spring,

of not waking to the glassy-eyed monstrous heads
the staggering, shattered people, newly dead.

At last I was away from the furious dead
and the deadening lives and back to the land of the living

freer, more carefree than ever,
the wind in my black hair, my dark eyes clear.

By Lake Oguta

I went to where the Lake Oguta
meets the Orashi River.

I thought of reading *Efuru*
years ago by Flora Nwapa

and of all the roads that led to here.
The river ran into Lake Oguta

but did not mix its waters;
I could see as clear as clear

the tea brown of the Orashi River
the bright blue of Lake Oguta.

Not so far from here, the River Niger,
not so far, the Niger Delta,

not so far from Imo State, Anambra,
not so far from here, my father.

I have travelled the roads and the miles;
I've crossed the rivers and lakes;

I have landed on African soil
for the second time. I've got what it takes.

The country holds out its brown hands,
the lake allows me to draw some water.

Later tonight, I will eat till I am full,
some fish, some yam and some cassava.

Holy Island

All winter I was waiting
for something to give
and today I felt it,
a small crack,
the sun on the sandy dunes
by the Causeway,
the feeling of the land
so close to the sea.
Nick and me and the dog
striding along
by the old Benedictine monastery
till we walked into
a new vocabulary –
hope, benevolence, benediction –
after the long wintering
of false starts,
the same day over and over,
the spring at last here –
I said a small prayer,
the wind in my hair.

The Bird

i.m. Julia Darling

Coming in, only now, as if released like that bird,
the story of the bird,
as if something earlier, the cold hands of grief
had double-locked the door and put on the chain.
Yet now the back door is miraculously open:
you are up, surprised to be walking again

into this cottage, a mug of tea in your hand.
Since you've been gone, you've become a grandmother.
Something strange happened to time:
it got longer, and shorter; it was numbered: numb.
And when once it hurt to think of you dead

now you move at ease around in my head.

21st Birthday Poem for Matthew

Matthew, I remember
before you were born, I felt you
dancing in my waters –
turning and twisting and flipping –
and how just after the Sunday afternoon
you came into my world,
you danced to Handel's Water Music,
as you always had,
a fluid watery dance.

And now twenty-one years on,
you are still dancing underwater, my son,
with stingrays and yellow fins
barracudas and marlins,
finding in the deep mystery of the sea
something of that tranquillity
I imagine you loved as a tiny baby.

Now you swim between shoals of tuna –
closer than the imagination,
those vivid colours –
and the water parts its magic hands
as you, my bold adventurer son,
take the whole wide world in your own fine hands.

Muse

You cannot hear a poem coming,
its wings as soundless as a night-moth's,
or call it to heel or follow as you would a dog.
It is not biddable, it has no tomorrow, and it won't fly in
even if you leave your window wide open.

You might not even see it coming,
small as it sometimes is – a fly,
an ant, a ladybird – or big as it sometimes is –
a rhino, an elephant in the room, a hippopotamus.
The muse sneaks into your house by stealth

like a burglar, slides into your kitchen,
pours a glass of water – cool as you like –
by the sink, sneaks a look in your breadbin.
It has your number written on its hand.
It thinks it knows you well. It thinks it is your friend.

Missing You

(after *L'Étang des Sœurs* by Paul Cézanne)

I took you to the forest yesterday
where the trees breathed the same breath of sisters in their sleep,
the lush greenness like the deepest dream, like a memory:
the time when we walked into the heart of the woods
– where were we? – me ahead, and you following.
And then we borrowed a kiss from the edge of the woods,
and planted it on each other's lips, a kiss for good;
the trees, our witness, the leaves listening to our pledge.

And there you are again, today, beyond the body of that tree,
bending willingly towards me, as you were the time
you fell forward into my open arms,
the great bough of me ready for you, outstretched,
open as the heart is in the woods –
alive to your secrets, hidden in the foliage.
How long the age before you met me:
how long the age before I met you.

Now, here in the Dutton Valley, far from Osny,
up the road from the old bridge, past two cattle grids,
you are everywhere I am:
in bed this morning, I imagined I could see you
through the window on the farm road
to Beckfoot, behind the wooden gate,
turning the bend of the country road,
by the woods, by the stop of this tree

that reminds me of *L'Étang des Sœurs* by Cézanne –
arriving, suddenly here, girlfriend: the cottage in the hills,
your skin an autumn glow, your waving arms,
your chestnut hair falling over your face,
the rustle of your clothes as I undress you.
This is a conjurer's trick: here you are, my love,
walking through the secret woods to this cottage here
– down the low path, through the front door towards the open fire.

Fiere Love Poem

The nicht I kent oor love
wad go on and on and on, darlin,
the clouds mirrored the moth
we fund in the fields
at the back o' the butt an' ben –

then a fishbone, a skeleton,
as if a' thing kid be
paired doon to the wan essential,
so that ivery time I say
I love ye tae bits
you reply *I love ye to hale.*

Marigowds

Fir I will bring ye marigowds, my fiere –
ye who whaur there when I needed ye,
ye who are still hail and fere
though you've had a rough auld year.

Yer face is still fair farrant,
and the licht the day is licht farrant.
You've come frae the haird pairt like a farandman;
thru this dreich winter ye stole a piece o' ma hert.

The Marriage of Nick and Edward

When you get home from your wedding, dear boys,
and you've exchanged your plain and beautiful bands
– rose-gold with platinum for Nick,
rose-gold with gold for Edward –
and held together your handsome hands,
and kissed, and pledged a life of happiness,
I suggest you get out the quaich,
your special two-handled drinking bowl –
made of pewter, for your gifted future –
and pour some *Hallelujah* into the loving cup
and knock back the rose-gold liquid
and drink up, drink up, drink up!

Here are your years stretching ahead,
and the rose-gold love of the newly wed.

Valentine

On our first Valentine's
you appeared at precisely the same time
as me, on those cobbled streets
by the Quay, Castlefields,
as if you had loved me
all of my life already.

And our love was a castle and a field.

On our second Valentine's
I made a single bowl of tagolini
with shaved white truffle
and truffle oil
and though you had a cold – or was it me? –
we twirled and spun
our durum wheat round a silver spoon
before going to bed
and spinning and twirling again,
and later, sleeping like spoons.

And our love woke to a dream of ourselves years ahead.

On our third Valentine's
we went to *That Café* in Levenshulme
and you looked at me as if
I were the only girl in the room
and I could picture you then, your smile,
suddenly as an old woman.

And our love had walked the years like miles.

Tonight, the stars are out for us
dancing in the February cold
and our love is as young as it is old.

Castletown, Isle of Man

How strange the way old lovers move into the present,
tense, and catch you off guard; you tell me
when you were here last you'd taken the steam train to a place
whose name you've forgotten, and found a tapas bar.
Going to that island is like going back to the past.

Once we would have drunk a glass of red together
in the Garrison, or waved in unison at the mother
and child in that back garden waving at this steam train.
I see what you mean, I think to myself, *I see what you mean*,
waving on my own to the time before I was born.

These days we travel to the same places alone:
first you, then me, to this small, half-way island.
I pick up your scent round the narrow cobbled streets,
the medieval castle grounds, through the Market Square:
I stare at the dreamy boats coming into the harbour,

then conjure you, my ex-lover, in the Old House of Keys:
walking along the long and dimly-lit corridor,
across the stone floor – candle in hand – to friendship
carrying the low flame of the past, still flickering, just the same,
into the present, to the place that has no satisfactory name.

85th Birthday Poem for Dad

Last night on the eve of my father's birthday
I watched, from the bench by the sea in Erin Bay,
a large red sun fall behind the cliff,
ever so slowly, like a ball in a penalty.
Later, the moon smashed into the clouds –
a goal from the past lobbed into the present.
I remembered how my father's only bugbear
with my mother, his wife of over fifty years,
was how she never watched him play football
years ago, when he was centre forward
in the South Island of New Zealand.

And with the red sun and the full moon
so close in time in the sky's great pitch,
I found myself thinking of the way
my father used to dance across the ballroom floor
like Fred Astaire, or how he climbed the Munros,
and of how time is so fast and so slow.
I raised my half-pint glass –
my half-full glass –
then my extra wee half in his honour
a nippy whisky, *a Port Ellen*, my mother's name.

A half and a half or a *hauf and a hauf,*
the best way on this night away
to toast his health. 'Happy Birthday,'
I say to John Robert Kay.
If he were here on the Isle of Man
he'd already be thinking associatively:
Thomas Paine, Rights of Man.
Nobility is not hereditary, aye.
But he is not here, and so I raise
my nearly-drained glass to the empty sky.

Moon over Mexico

The night the volcano erupted in Iceland
the sunset here was eerily beautiful,
like those in your photographs.
Later, when I realised I couldn't go to Mexico,
the moon was the shape of a hammock
or that grey corduroy chair
you used to love bouncing in when you were a toddler,
or the eyebrow of a polar bear.

I asked myself to think of a colour for the sunset –
cherry blossom, candy floss, tequila,
none of it was any good, my eye was shot,
my ear was tin, I wasn't going to Guadalajara,
or to meet Eric or Lola. My head was stuffed with clichés.
All over the world people were missing their honeymoons
or funerals or dying words or last smiles.
I wondered if you could see in Mexico
exactly the same moon that I could see.
Write a poem, Mum, you said when
we found I definitely couldn't come.
I'll try, I cried, my eyelids thick as slugs.

One day, I thought, we'll go to Guadalajara together,
and look at the same sun and the same moon
in the Mexican sky, and all of this sadness
will seem light years away . . . That's as far
as I could get. Not even a decent simile.

My Mother Remembers Sri Lanka

Then there was thon time I was in Sri Lanka.
I'd never been the length of myself before.
And I'd never seen a coconut before.
And one of the Party men climbed the coconut tree,
knocked it down – dear me, what was I, nineteen?
It was like a dream, the things I'd never seen.
I just jumped at everything new! I saw a snake charmer!
He was a right warmer, and when they didn't let our driver
– he was in the party too – into the bar
well, we didn't go either. But, oh, Sri Lanka. Sri Lanka . . .
Mind you, it was Ceylon then. What's the capital, no, not Jakarta,
that's somewhere else althegither – Colombo!
Like thon detective with the mankie raincoat and fat cigar.
What a time I had in Sri Lanka! The coconut didn't taste of much,
but everything else was a wonder. *Oh Helen had a ball!*
When I saw that snake charmer
he told me the love of my life was near; so he is still.
Dear John, fifty odd years on – for our sins! I'm telling you.
I'm not having you on. Life isn't as long as it looks on the tin.

Green House

What pleasure it gives my mother aged eighty,
this greenhouse built by my brother,
where she grows her own tomatoes,
spicy leaves, chillies, courgettes.
And every day that she goes out
to slide open the glass door, no matter the weather,
and water her tomatoes – *do they soak up water* –
is another day on earth and *hallelujah!*
What joy, my tomatoes going from green to red
my mother says, sliding the door closed.
She stops in her garden to water her azalea.
Struggling on her pins. *Look at that colour:*
I'd rather water my flower bed than be dead,
she quips with her Lochgelly humour.

Impromptu

'He begins again, without seeming to, so uncertain is the shape . . . We dream of a summer night and sit there waiting for the song of the nightingale.'

George Sand

I stood at the grand piano and turned the page.
I watched the century glitter and fade.
The lid of the piano, half-open,
changed shape, became a great heron.

It seemed nothing now could be unmade.
I lifted my eyes and saw the clouds take shape.
I played my life back, the Blue Note, Carmen Macrae;
the music took me round the world in days.

I saw Chopin shake hands with Abdullah Ibrahim
and heard the voice from my dream last night say,
'Nobody plays like Abdullah Ibrahim!'
And time slipped and fell away.

The piano notes became the sea, rippling waves.
Once, I'd used the word FACE to help with the spaces.
I stood at the piano and I was all races.
And the music played past Ali Farka Toure.

Suddenly the night was all around me;
light clouds took the shape of lost loves.
It came like a revelation:
death is not the final curtain.

I had it in my head as a comforting thing:
when I die my son will play my heart's choice.
They will be alive, as they've always been,
Bessie Smith, Sarah Vaughan, Nina Simone.

Dark African Wood

(after Henry Moore)

I have come from the woods
from the small, lonely night.
I lost my baby; I couldn't have a baby.
My heart's as heavy as the wood that made me.

I remember the secret of the trees.
I was always running away, wind through me;
my heart beating through the woods, trying
to cross the black river, to be free.

It was night, dark night, never bright.
I couldn't run when the sun was high.
I passed a girl whose hands were clasped;
she stood as still as alabaster.

Each one of us is always alone.
All my life, I'll hear my baby crying –
the cry of the long lost in the wild.
I wish I had never been with child.

Road to Amaudo

(the village of peace in Igbo)

The road to Amaudo
like the road to Nzagha
like roads all over Nigeria
all over Africa
is a winding and long
red dust road
stretching
perhaps into infinity
to a foreseeable future
and back to
lost time:

the road to Amaudo
is at times impassable:
but pass people do,
men and women and children,
hefting the load
of hope on their backs
the frail weight of peace
on their shoulders,
round one corner
and then another,
round one bend, then the next:
a father, a daughter,
a mother, a son –
the good green of the elephant grasses
beside the deep red
like a constant companion,

a compadre, a fiere.
                    Come, let us go
down the road to Amadou
        and shake hands
                    with our old selves,
    the ones whose names
            we have forgotten,
                        who once were fragile,
    those people; *you*, *me*,
who have had felt the cracks, the crevices,
                    who were lost to their families
                            or lost to themselves.
    I want to walk on the road to Amadou,
            the road to my heart,
            like a road I once walked down,
        like the road to Nzagha,
ka udo di, ka ndu di.

The No-Longer Dead

The people who are no longer dead,
who were so cold in their skin, so unlike their old selves,
have returned to the living rooms and kitchens
fields and gardens, beaches and benches,
streets, bus stops, cafes; all their favoured places.

How surprising it is, when you go to cut the hedge
or cut back the cherry blossom tree, or water the clematis,
or retile the roof, or buy from the deli some strong cheese –
how strange and pleased you are to find them coming too,
no longer gaunt; nothing left of that old disease.

Back, the long-ago-deceased, they've put weight on,
and are hanging around the old haunts,
having their open-ended conversation. You can even hear a laugh.
The voice you thought you had forgotten
has returned, with almost the same intonation.

Dear friends, you find yourself saying, *over the moon!*

Bronze Head from Ife

Open the granite gneiss, my friend,
and tak yer share o' happiness.
Forget the auld days o' disgrace,
locked in the lang gone since.
Crunch yer kola nut fir luck.
It's time tae raise yer heid.
Look into yer ain een, startling,
defiant. Examine the hole in yer chin,
the caved-in bit o' yer face.
Ye tak the words frae my tongue.
Looking back and furward in time,
ye could hae been forgotten,
dug up, as ye were, by accident:
but naw, ye're here and a' een
are on your een that hae seen a' things
– even when yer back wis turned,
yer een had the talent o' the chameleon;
ye've been here and ye've been gone
sin auld lang syne. Gies yer haund!
Miracle that ye are, yer braw face
lifts my heart; naebody can doot yer art.
I would hae loved tae ken yer maister;
I wid hae liked to ken his name.
Mind hoo at first they thoucht ye were
fray the Lost Atlantis. They couldnie
credit ye, made fray
zinc and brass and loss.
Inside the granite gneiss,
you'll clock the shocking past, the sadnesses,

the ships, the human clearances.
But noo, it's time tae raise yer gless!
Tak a cup o' kindness yet.
Here's tae the return o' the long lost!
Here's tae ye, thing o' beauty!
Yer no a mask; yer no a disguise.
Here's tae that timeless look in yer eyes.

Fiere Good Nicht

(after Gussie Lord Davis)

When you've had your last one for the road,
a Linkwood, a Talisker, a Macallan.
And you've finished your short story,
and played one more time *Nacht und Träume*,
with Roland Hayes singing sweetly;
and pictured yourself on the road,
the one that stretches to infinity,
and said goodnight to your dead,
and fathomed the links in the long day –

then it's time to say Goodnight fiere,
and lay your highland head on your feather pillow,
far away – in England, Canada, New Zealand –
and coorie in, coorie in, coorie in.
The good dreams are drifting quietly doon,
like a figmaleerie, my fiere, my dearie,
and you'll sleep as soond as a peerie,
and turn, turn slowly towards the licht:
goodnight fiere, fiere, Good Nicht.

Glossary

Fiere

thegither – together

braw – fine, splendid

cauld – cold

blithe – in good spirits, cheerful

blatter – babble

bonny – pretty

blether – conversation

barrie – fine

Igbo Bath

Igbo – Nigerian tribe

Odene – oldest person in the village

Granite

quine – a girl, a young unmarried woman

loon – a fellow, chap, lad

haar – east-coast sea fog

stane – stone

alane – alone

richt – right

fray – from

gin – by the time that, in readiness for, so there will be

Brockit

brocket, brocked, brucket – (adj) 1. black and white
    stripes or spots of an animal, esp. a cow or sheep
    having a white streak down its face. 2. (of oats) black
    and white oats growing together

unco' – very much

dreich – dreary, bleak, dull

sleekit – sly, cunning, not to be trusted

pleassour – pleasure

brockle – a cross-bred sheep from a Leicester ram and a
blackface ewe; flecked, streaked.

Egusi Soup

magi – stock cube

ugwu – pumpkin leaves

Body o' Land

harebells – the round-leaved bell-flower, the bluebell of
Scotland

bothy – rough hut used as temporary accommodation, a
separate building on a farm

nicht – night

licht – light

thrawn – twisted, distorted

selkie – seals that can shed their skins to become humans

from A Drunk Woman Looks at her Nipple

fou – drunken

muckle – much

deid dune – done in

spit o' – the double of, the exact likeness

hinkie-pinkie – lopsided

fu – full

havering – nonsensical, talking nonsense

ain – one

ken – know

Kamso, Kedu

Kedu – how are you

quaich – a shallow bowl-shaped drinking cup, made of
    pewter or silver
Slàinte mhath – to your good health, cheers

Burying My African Father
Odimma – fine, thank you

Fiere Love Poem
kent – knew
wad – would
butt n' ben – small house
hale – whole

Marigowds
marigowds – marigolds
hail and fere – healthy, sturdy
fair farrant – handsome, attractive, pleasant appearance
licht farrant – frivolous
haird – hard
farandman – travelling person

My Mother Remembers Sri Lanka
thon – that
warmer – character
althegither – altogether
mankie – dirty, to be found wanting

Road to Amaudo
ka udo di, ka ndu di – let there be peace, let there be life

Bronze Head from Ife
een – eyes
sin auld lang syne – since days gone by
Tak a cup o' kindness – from Burns' 'Auld Lang Syne'

Fiere Good Nicht

Nacht und Träume – night and dreams
coorie in – tuck in
coorie – the stables of the royal household
figmaleerie – a whim, a fanciful notion
peerie – a small stone marble

Notes and Acknowledgements

'Fiere' was commissioned by the Scottish Poetry Library and first published in *25 poets respond to Burns*.

'The Returning' originally appeared in the *Poetry Review*, December 2010.

'Black River' was inspired by attending the Calabash Poetry Festival in Jamaica, and first published in *Wasafiri*.

'Lament for the Mendi Men' – The *Mendi* was a steamship chartered by the British government which sank off the Isle of Wight in 1917 with the loss of six hundred and forty-six South African men. (Six hundred and seven black troops died in the disaster, the worst in South African maritime history.) The *Mendi* was transporting men from a South African battalion to France during World War One. The poem was commissioned by the BBC and first broadcast on a radio 4 documentary, *The Lament of the SS Mendi*.

'Woman at a Window' and 'Lady with a Parasol' were commissioned by the Courtauld Institute of Art and first published in the *Guardian*.

'A Drunk Woman Looks at her Nipple' was first published in *New Poems Chiefly in the Scottish Dialect* (Polygon) ed. Robert Crawford, as were 'Brockit' and 'Body o' Land'. The first line and the last two lines come from Hugh MacDiarmid's 'A Drunk Man Looks at the Thistle'.

'Windows, Lakes', was commissioned by the British Council.

'Strawberry Meringue' was commissioned by the Scottish Poetry Library.

'Twins' was inspired by the *Painted Truths* exhibition of Alice Neel at the Whitechapel Art Gallery.

'Dark African Wood' was written after visiting the Henry Moore exhibition at the Tate Britain. The title comes from a sculpture, *Composition 1932*, made in dark African wood. The girl with her hands clasped is made in Cumberland alabaster.

'Road to Amaudo' was inspired by the work of the small UK-based charity Amaudo, which provides mental-health care and community support over five states in south-eastern Nigeria.

'Bronze Head from Ife' came from the brilliant exhibition of the same name at the British Museum.

'Fiere Good Nicht' is inspired by the song 'Good Night Irene', which was in turn inspired by the original lyrics by Gussie Lord Davis, an African-American songwriter who wrote 'Irene, Good Night' in 1886 and was the first Black American writer to acquire fame on Tin Pan Alley.